Muhammad's Mountain

Homage to The Greatest

PoEMS

John Warner Smith

Lavender Ink
lavenderink.org

Muhammad's Mountain
John Warner Smith

Copyright © 2018 by the author and Diálogos Books.

All rights reserved. No part of this work may be reproduced
in any form without the express written permission
of the copyright holders and Diálogos Books.

Printed in the U.S.A.
First Printing
10 9 8 7 6 5 4 3 2 1   18 19 20 21 22 23

Book design: Bill Lavender
Front cover photo © Neil Leifer, Getty Images.
Author photo by Thomas Sayers Ellis.

Library of Congress Control Number: 2018945382
Smith, John Warner
Muhammad's Mountain / John Warner Smith;
p. cm.
ISBN: 978-1-944884-43-7 (pbk.)

Lavender Ink
lavenderink.org

Acknowledgments

Grateful acknowledgment is made to the editors and readers of the following journals where poems in this collection have appeared or are forthcoming:

Concho River Review	"Shadowboxing"
Ellipsis	"Brother Malcolm"
Jelly Bucket	"Renaissance Man"
Kestrel	"Parkinson's" "Afghanistan"
Louisiana Cultural Vistas	"Mirage" "Shadow"
MockingHeart Review	"Finding God" "In the Wake"
Natural Bridge	"Last Bell" "The Negro Athlete and the Racial Mountain"
Obsidian: Literature & Arts in the Diaspora	"Legend"
Pembroke Magazine	"Belief" "Cosell" "Bundini"
Plume	"Louisville"
Quiddity	"Louisville Lip"
St. Petersburg Review	"Son of Africa"
The Louisville Review	"Black Power"
The McNeese Review	"Liminal"
The Missouri Review	"The Torch"
The Wayne Literary Review	"Big Time Buck White"

Contents

Seeking God

For The Greatest

Nobody can give you freedom.
Nobody can give you equality or justice or anything.
If you're a man, you take it.

—Malcolm X, *Malcolm X Speaks: Selected Speeches and Statements*

Muhammad's Mountain

One Life

Some stories are lived to be told
as a journey in the light

> of one day,
> one glorious rising
> and setting of the sun,

when one life,

> with all its beauty and bravado
> > blazing the gray, blanketing clouds
> > and bone-chilling air,

forever touches our lives

with conviction
to freedom, justice, and peace.

Boxing, Religion, and Politics

Shadowboxing

Like staring in the mirror
at the Catholic school where you swept floors,
you couldn't get past the face
of Emmett Till, a black boy nearly your age,
who went down South
and was lynched
for whistling at a white woman,

     his pretty face

     and the one lying in the glass-covered coffin,
     mutilated and bloated with gouged eyes.

All you could do was shadowbox:

     derail a train car with shoe shine rests
     you had stolen from Aunt Eva's Barber Shop,

     and throw rocks at a goateed "Uncle Sam"
     wearing a striped suit and star-studded top hat,
     pointing his finger at you.

But you knew there would come a time
when the fight bell would ring.

Mirage

I picture the fiery red sparkle
of a Schwinn Hornet bicycle,

your first Cadillac, gleaming
in your wide, beckoning eyes,

you leaning forward and low,
pedaling fast as a jet propeller

into a soft Kentucky wind,
the turbulent sky of Jim Crow

merely a shimmering mirage
on the hot asphalt road. Then,

Emmett Till, Rosa Parks, Rome,
a hero's welcome in Louisville,

and "We don't serve Negroes."
Your Olympic gold tarnished,

its spangled ribbon tightening
like a noose around your neck,

you on a bridge seeing America
sink into the Ohio River.

Little Lonnie's Angel

Little, shy, first-grade girl,
freckled, snaggle-toothed, pig-tailed girl,
Marguerite Williams, Louisville, Verona Way girl,
    Cassius, Olympic champ, is in town today,
    across the street, visiting his mama.
    Stop hiding behind your mama's dress, girl.
    Go with the boys, talk to the champ.
    He's fun; he'll make you laugh.

See. Told you, cute huh? He's the one,
a little loud, cocky, and wide-eyed, not your age,
but he's the one. Wait and see.

His sun is rising. It'll be bright and golden
all by itself. One day, he'll shine for all
the world to see. Everyone will know
his name and face. You'll see.

He's a boxer, you know, the best ever,
and he already knows it. Nobody told him;
he just knows he's the greatest fighter of all time,
and he's not even the heavyweight champ yet.
But you wait and see. He'll shake up the world.

There's something different about him.
He brags about the beauty of his blackness.
He prays to God every day and feels a spirit
inside him that he knows is greater than him
and bigger than anything or anyone outside

of him. He's no saint. He battles demons
and loses. But he keeps his eyes on the prize.
His faith, that's his power. He's living a dream.

But in his dream there is a mountain,
a tall rock that appears out of nowhere
and stands in his path.
He can't move that mountain,
can't get around it.
No river can flow through it.
His sunlight doesn't glow.

Like all humans, he is dying
from the moment of birth.
Beyond the mountain
is where his God is,
a place where he'll never die.
That's where he wants to be,
at the top of that rock.
He wants to see God.

He knows that kindness and love
will get him there,
but there are storms along the way,
valleys he must cross.
He can't get there on his own.
You can help him.
I know you can.
Sure, you're young, have things to do,
places to go, a life to live.
But don't you already know

how much you love him,
how you can help him to see God?
Yes, of course you do.

The Greatest

I'm on top of the world.
I'm the greatest thing that ever lived.
I'm so great, I don't have a mark on my face,
    and I just upset Sonny Liston,
    and I'm only 22 years old.
I must be the greatest.

I told the world I talk to God every day.
If God's with me, can't nobody be against me.
I shook up the world.
I know God.
I know the real God.

I'm king of the world.
I'm pretty.
I'm a baaaad man.
I shook up the world.
I shook up the world.
I shook up the world.
I can't be beat.

I AM THE GREATEST.

Minutes after winning the heavyweight crown on February 25, 1964, in what Joe Louis called the biggest upset in the history of boxing, an exuberant Cassius Clay, still in the ring with gloves on, shouted these words into a commentator's microphone. And the legend began.

Belief

You naturally stood above most men,
    but when you had them lock-jawed
        under the spell of your dance,

your hands low, head bobbing,
    jabs buzzing like a bee,

        the magic kicked in.

Like the ghost punch
    that turned Liston's lights out
        and dropped him to the canvas,

your best combination was unseen,
    not left-right thunder and flash

        but belief in believing,

swelling your child-like heart.
    In that moment, every knee bent,

        every power outside your God fell.

I Am America

We want freedom by any means necessary.
We want justice by any means necessary.
We want equality by any means necessary.
—Malcolm X, June 28, 1964

1964.

America still dreaming nightmares
of 1963:
    a slain U.S. president,
    four black girls killed by the bombing
        of a Birmingham church.
Mississippi Civil Rights leader
        Medgar Evers gunned down
        at his front door.

1964.

A shepherd boy shook up the world,
killed a giant with a sling and one stone,
America's new heavyweight golden boy,
the Louisville Lip,
the total package—young, handsome, strong,
floats like a butterfly, stings like a bee,
and Christian until he said,

I don't have to be what you want me to be.
I'm free to be who I want.

I'm not the white man's slave
    and I don't want his name.
I'm Cassius X.
I'm black.
I'm Muslim
    and I follow the teachings
    of the Honorable Elijah Muhammad:
        Black don't need white to be what it is.
        Black don't need white to be equal.
        Black is free.
        Black is beautiful.
        Black is God's children.

I'm Muhammad Ali.

I am America.
I am the part you won't recognize.
But get used to me—black, confident, cocky;
my name, not yours;
my religion, not yours;
my goals, my own.
Get used to me.

Voices

Champ, you really are King of the World,
everything for your taking—fame, cars,
women, anything money can buy.

This is America, 1964, Negroes fighting
for voting rights and racial integration,
Negro leaders beaten, jailed, dying
for justice and equality. You're a boxer,
world champ, only 22, our hero.
Imagine what you can do
for your people, for Negro children.
Look at Jackie, Floyd and Joe,
the examples they set.

Why

Cassius X,
the day after winning the crown,

the Nation of Islam
and its hate-spewing words,

Malcolm x,
the most hated Negro in America?

Why

Muhammad Ali and not Cassius Clay,
the good-looking, clean-cut Christian kid
from Louisville with a big smile
and golden hands, our darling boy
of sports who fought his way to the top?

Renaissance Man

After Liston, they fell like dominoes:
Folley, Terrell, Williams, Mildenberger,
London, Cooper, Chuvalo, and Patterson,
dizzied by his lightning quick jabs
and the waltz of his dazzling white shoes,
sparkling like chrome
as he bicycled across the canvas.

We stood witness to the creation
of modern day myth—Black Superman
from Krypton, Kentucky,
undefeated god of the ring,
clairvoyant and charismatic,
denigrating and taunting challengers

while staring into his crystal ball.

He wanted to go to heaven so I beat him in seven.
It ain't no jive, he'll go in five.
He might be great but he'll fall in eight.

Ali vernacular.
Ali meter.
Ali rhyme.

Ali renaissance:
    black beauty,
    black ballet,
    black poetry
    on the wings of a butterfly,

with foot work, hand speed, and power
that whupped ass.

Louisville Lip

We wear the mask that grins and lies,
It hides our cheeks and shades our eyes,—
This debt we pay to human guile;
With torn and bleeding hearts we smile,
And mouth with myriad subtleties.
    —Paul Lawrence Dunbar, "We Wear the Mask"

Cassius created you, the actor
    who spun his own silky satin persona
    with a mouthful of words—loud, audacious
    doggerel and trash talk,

        signifying, prophesying,
        and stirring up the amen corner,

    just in time for prime time,
    magazine cover stories,
    and talcum-splashing barbershop big talk.

He styled you like
    Gorgeous George without curls and capes,
    Fred Astaire in Pat Boone shoes,
        high-top and polished,
    Sugar Ray Robinson dishing out the salt.

Fans loved the circus clown
and the Mardi Gras mask
    in a king's coronation
with brass horns and bass drums
bringing up the rear.

One character, many faces,
    but Ali always brought the mojo
    to back you up.

Induction (April 28, 1967, Houston)

I.

King Muhammad, come down from your throne.
Step forward, be American.
Be rock and resolute.
Be Army.
      Step.
      Step.
      Step up, Muhammad.
Time to shuffle, dance, and float for America.

Say a poem now, pretty boy.
Lift your voice and sing
for the sweet land of liberty.

"rockets' red glare, the bombs bursting in air."

      Preach now, Muslim man, fisher-man.
      Step up!
      Shake up the world.

Put down your hand-held mirror, Muhammad.
Stand at attention.
Salute.
Take this gun.
Kill for your country.

II.

NO

NO to the white man's war
NO to the white man's God
NO to the white man's laws
NO to the white man's injustice
NO to the white man's inequality
NO to the white man's bigotry and hatred
NO to the white man speaking for black people
NO to the white man beating and lynching
      innocent black boys and men
NO to the white man bombing churches
      and killing innocent black girls
NO to the white man raping black women
NO to the white man burning crosses
      and terrorizing black people
NO to being the white devil's Uncle Tom

NO, I will not go 10,000 miles from here
to help murder and kill another poor people
simply to continue the domination
of white slave masters
over the darker people of the earth.

Cosell

To say the name you had to wrap your mind around it,
bury sound in a black hole, think sooner or later
it will be passé, like afro, medallion, and dashiki.
Cassius, the kid from Louisville with golden hands,
now heavyweight champ of the world.
Muslim? Nation of Islam?
Cosell said it: *Your name is Muhammad Ali.*

"Get that nigger-loving Jew bastard off the air,"
one hate letter read, when Cosell later defended
Ali's stand against the draft,
but the ex-lawyer,
quintessential sports critic
and broadcaster kept defending,
nasal Brooklyn accent,
toupee and all.

When you saw them on television,
facing off one on one, firing back and forth,
you stopped, listened, turned up the volume,
and watched them jab, hook, and hit
below the belt—two tar babies
tangling, giving each other the sticky,
feeding off warm, bright lights
and the love between them.

The Trial (June 20, 1967, Houston)

a man   a name   a race   a religion

a minister   a boxer   a champion

a country

a war

a military

a system of racial inequality

a summer on fire

a minister   a boxer   a champion

a man   a name   a race   a religion

a charge of refusing induction

a trial in the south

a white jury

a white judge

a deliberation of 1,260 seconds

a verdict of guilty

a man   a name   a race   a religion

a minister   a boxer   a champion

Message from the United States of America to its Young Black Men

There's battle lines being drawn
Nobody's right if everybody's wrong
    —Buffalo Springfield, "For What It's Worth"

So there you have it.
Five years in prison and a $10,000 fine.
A warrior without a cause,
a champion without a crown, without honor
and the millions he would have earned.
Once a shining morning star,
now a speck of dust
on the hall of sports immortality.

Let Ali be a lesson to every thug
and holy-rolling draft dodger
in America. Whether you're under
the mattress or behind the cloth,
the law has no respect of persons.
We will win. You will lose,
and you'll pay the ultimate price
for refusing to serve your country.

Voices II

There's something strangely inconsistent
about a nation and a press that will praise you
when you say be non-violent toward Jim Clark,
but will curse and damn you when you say
be non-violent toward little brown Vietnamese children.
       —Dr. Martin Luther King, Jr., April 30, 1967

Remember what they did to Malcolm, Martin, and
    Bobby?
When you speak out against the government
and war, they'll shut you up
with a bullet.

Ali, what does it profit a man
to gain the world and lose his own soul?

You cannot serve two masters.

You're not alone in this fight.
You're on the side of truth and justice.

Go on, brother.
Stand your ground against war.
Hold fast to your beliefs.
Give up the world, your life if necessary.
Follow your moral compass, trust it
beyond reason, beyond sight,
beyond the promise of success.

Never mind the haters,

the doubters and pincers.
Go on, strong man. Let your light shine.
Speak out. Show the world
who you are, what you believe.

The Negro Athlete and the Racial Mountain

I ain't no Langston Hughes. I'm a boxer.
And I ain't saying these so-called Negro athletes
who don't respect my beliefs want to be white,
but they sure sound white
when they say I'm wrong for being Muslim, wrong
for doing away with my slave name,
and wrong for refusing to go 10,000 miles
to kill innocent brown people for America
when America won't even fight for me
and my people right here at home. Jackie Robinson,
Floyd Patterson, Ernie Terrell, Joe Lewis,
they're the white man's champions.
I'm the champion of the people, the ones
down in Parkland and Southside Chicago
and Harlem, the ones who can't even afford
a ticket or a television to see me fight.

I don't live and fight for the white man's acceptance.
I'm free to be whoever I want to be,
because Allah gives me the courage, strength,
and wisdom to beat anybody who stands
between me and the championship of the world.
As far as Patterson and Terrell are concerned,
I took my time to punish them,
because they wouldn't call me by my name,
and they should have known better.
If they was white, I would have had compassion

and ended both fights sooner.
But as so-called Negroes, they should have
shown respect for a black man
who was fighting for justice and equality.
So I had to punish them. In fact, if Joe Lewis
wasn't so old and could climb back into the ring,
I'd whip him just as bad.

I ain't saying all black athletes is Uncle Toms.
Some of the top athletes in the world—Jim Brown,
Bill Russell, Lew Alcindor—they support my stand
against the war. These are what I call
real champions, not them so-called Negroes
who try to sound white
or duck, hide, and keep their mouths shut
in order not to offend the white man.

Ain't no fighter greater than me.
White folks didn't make me who I am.
To the contrary, they're trying to destroy me
inside and outside the ring.
Took my title. Won't let me fight.
Broke my bank account.
Trying to lock me up and destroy me,
just because I don't believe in war
and refuse to fight them Viet Cong.

But I'm walking to the beat of my own drum,
not the white man's music. I'm black

and pretty and the greatest heavyweight
champion of all time. I don't fight and live
to please white people or to be like them.
I'm on top of the mountain, praise be to Allah,
and I got here by being true
to who I am—a black man and a Muslim.

Symbols of Un-Americanism in the Psyche of White Americans (1964-1968)

Stokely Carmichael
H. Rap Brown
Elijah Muhammad
Malcolm X
Amiri Baraka

Tommie Smith
John Carlos
Eldridge Cleaver
Huey Newton
Bobby Seale

Muhammad Ali

His anti-whiteness mistaken
to mean "hate"—something feared.

Only love, a blindness to color,
could have seen that Ali only meant

"black, something beautiful,
people to be loved."

Exile and Return

Cassius Marcellus Clay

Fighters, survivors, champions of freedom and
    equality. Surely, as lions, their two paths crossed:
a political rally or convention, maybe a midnight
    barn gathering along the Underground Railroad.
Frederick Douglass meeting Cassius Marcellus Clay,
    the wealthy Kentucky farmer and abolitionist
whose name was given to your father and you,
    the "slave name" you later abandoned.
Perhaps, in their brief encounters they talked
    news—politics of Lincoln and Civil War—or
shared stories of cunning runaway escapes,
    bomb threats, and fist fights. Ali, "beloved of God,"
in some ways you never stopped being Cassius.

Belinda

Ali, when day sky darkened,
   strong winds swirled
      and the ground below you

started to quake, Allah
   sent Belinda, a flower
      whose stem didn't bend

and petals didn't fall. Not long
   after the Olympic gold,
      years before she bloomed,

she stepped out of a dream,
   crossing your path
      like a child of innocence,

speaking like a mirror
   for the self unseen,
      the man you could become,

her sepal growing
   to gird your body,
      one day guard your soul.

Word Power

Boxing had been your school since the age of 12.
Then, at 25, you got locked out of the ring,
and had to go toe to toe with Phi Beta Kappas
to earn a living and prove there was reason
in your rhyme. You and Belinda in the Cadillac,
crisscrossing America to college campuses
and television talk shows. No slippery dance
and jab, just fist-words from your talking book,
raw, unplugged and unfiltered.

You my enemy, not no Chinese, no Vietcong, no Japanese.
You my opposer when I want freedom.
You my opposer when I want justice.
You my opposer when I want equality.
Want me to go somewhere and fight for you?
You won't even stand up for me right here in America,
for my rights and my religious beliefs.
You won't even stand up for my rights here at home.

Ali, with war raging for the soul of your race,
cities blazing with protest and resistance,
words were bullets. With a microphone
at your mouth, who could match your wit,
bravado and improvisation. Who could doubt
your conviction to principle? Your trumpet
solo soared "Miles in the Sky."

Big Time Buck White

Wasn't the first time
a black American superstar athlete
had to step out of his game
to earn a buck. When Jesse Owens
came home from Berlin
with four gold medals,
he was spotted forty yards
and barely beat Julio McGraw,
a Cuban thoroughbred.
When they barred Ali
from the ring for three years,
he took center stage,
Ali style, on Broadway,
under glittering neon lights,
raising Cassius out of the grave
to become Big Time Buck White,
a fake afro, fake beard-wearing
cutout of the Black Arts Movement,
singing and proselytizing
social justice and black liberation.
Hearing him sing "We Came in Chains,"
half-song, half-spoken word,
our feet tapped,
heads rocked back and forth,
and if we'd been in church,
somebody would have shouted
amen or *preach brother.*

It was all acting, a paycheck
that ended too soon,
but when the final curtain fell,
we knew we had heard Ali.

Super Fight

Let me tell you, boy, I was there,
not in person, but I saw that fight.
No buildup. No ringside crowd,
just Marciano and Clay, the only two
undefeated heavyweight champs.
I remember that night like yesterday.
January 20, 1970. Snowed all day.
Your grandma and I had to push
the pickup to get it going.

Marciano whipped Clay's butt,
plain and simple.
Knocked him out in the 13th round.
Next day, Clay came out and called it fake.
Said the fight was some kind of computer
made in Alabama. Said he and Rocky
only sparred a few rounds
and the computer did the rest. Said
he only did it 'cause he needed the money.
Bull! The fight was real
and Clay got a real ass whipping.
Rocky beat him to a pulp.

People say Clay was soft and slow,
'cause he hadn't fought for couple of years.
He looked pretty fit to me.
Clay was, what? 27?
Marciano was 45, 45 years old!
He had trimmed down quite a bit,

and it looked like he had a toupee,
but Clay couldn't hit hard enough
to knock it off. Clay was, what, 6 foot 3?
The tallest man Marciano ever fought.
Rocky chopped him down to a stump.
Rocky was short, so he didn't have much
reach. Not much footwork either,
but he didn't need it.
His hands did the job,
like a hammer on a fence post.
Had Clay on the run all night, the way
he did Jersey Joe Walcott and Archie Moore.
Marciano bled a little, and Clay got lucky
and knocked him down once,
but Rocky got right back up
and went at Clay like a freight train.
I heard the punch when he hit Clay
on the jaw with Suzie Q.
That's what he called his right hand
killer punch. Then he caught Clay
with a left. Clay went to his knees
and tried to pull himself up
with the ropes. TKO baby!

The fight was filmed. Then,
Marciano died in a plane crash,
so they only showed it one time,
at the drive-in. Rocky never
got to see it but he died knowing
he was the greatest of all time.
And you know what's really sweet?

He was one of us. Not from Texas,
an Italian boy, but still red-blooded,
and he wasn't out there mouthing off
and talking bad about good white people.
Some folks tried to make Clay
out to be some kind of hero,
'cause he dodged the draft
and didn't go to Viet Nam.
Damn coward. That's what he was.
They should have locked him up.
Computer. Bull!

Black Power

October 1970. Jackson 5 tops the charts.
    Ali three years without a fight. Like a buzzard,
        jail time hovers over his head. Tonight,

the ring is his stage again, black drama
    on the big screen in badass, blaxploitation fashion.
        Ali coming back. Quarry, the latest Great White Hope,

a hired dream killer. But this is Muhammad Ali
    after three years in exile. This is Atlanta, GA, where
        black dreams come true, on a night

when blackness steps out dressed to kill. Black actors,
    athletes, singers, pimps, preachers, prostitutes,
        and politicians—all panache, all here to see

The Greatest, cheer him on, hear his mouth,
        watch him float, duck, and jab. Ringside sideshows
        decked in mink, fur, diamonds and pearls.

This is Nation Time, Civil Rights, Black Power Time.
    And tonight, no one is blacker, prettier,
        more right and powerful than The Champ.

Shadow

Some days, moving flatfooted, naked,
retreating to the ropes,
you were pounded into submission,
beaten by your own shadow, TKO'd.
There had been no hype and doggerel
for those battles, fought underground,
away from lights, cameras, the glitz
and smoke of hollering fans. Only you
and Aphrodite in the pitch-black day.
Maybe you were just weak, Ali,
or the wild sweetness was toxic
enough to rock you senseless, oblivious
to the earthquake tremor at your feet.

Clay v. United States (June 28, 1971)

The final round has ended. The fight has ended. It's over!
Ladies and Gentlemen, may I have your attention, please?
Ladies and Gentlemen, we have a decision.
Nearly four years after he said,
"No, I will not go 10,000 miles
to help kill another poor people,"
nearly five years after he said
"I don't have no quarrel with them Viet Cong,"

after he was convicted, sentenced to five years
in prison, fined $10,000, stripped of his title
as heavyweight champion of the world,
and banned from the ring for over three years,

we have a decision:

Chief Justice Warren E. Burger scores every round Ali.
Justice Hugo Black scores it Ali.
Justice Harry Blackmun scores it all Ali.
Justice William J. Brennan, Jr.—Ali.
Justice William O. Douglas—every round Ali.
Justice John M. Harlan, II—all Ali.
Justice Potter Stewart scores all Ali.
Justice Byron White—Ali.
Justice Thurgood Marshall abstains.

The WINNER by unanimous decision,
"free at last, free at last,"
and still The Greatest,
the kid from Louisville
who shook up the world,
the Black Muslim Bomber,
Black Superman,
The baaaad maaaan
who has whupped President Richard Nixon,
Vice-President Spiro Agnew,
the U.S. Congress,
the U.S. Armed Forces,
and the U.S. Department of Justice,
all in one fight, one ring,
his religion scorned,
his hands and feet tied, and
his back pinned to the ropes,

still standing,
still Muslim,
still the People's Champ,
Muhammad Ali.
Aleeee!
Aleeee!
Aleeee!

Broken

Ali, that night in '73, when you stepped into the ring
to face Ken Norton, you looked more like
a rock & roll star than a fighter.
Maybe the rhinestone and gem-studded robe
that Elvis had given you
brought the jinx. Maybe you should have
taken Nobody Norton more serious.

Some fighters would have shouted,
"Hell no. This ain't fair," and called it quits
in the second round, the way Corky Baker,
the Central High School bully, had done
that day you took him on
in a three-rounder at Columbia Gym.
But you fought ten more rounds
after Norton's right hand broke your jaw,
round after round of blood gushing
up your throat, filling your mouth, eventually
shutting you up for post-fight interviews.

When the fight ended, Cosell described you
as *a beaten, broken fighter, once very great,*
but now a part of fistic history. We know now,
Champ, that for you and for boxing,
history had not even begun to be written.

Smokin' Joe

Joe, you knew there couldn't be
a fourth fight. Like Ali,
something in you died in Manila.

Some wounds never healed.
Ali once asked, "Where is Joe's pain,
why won't he fall?" Ali felt

your pain in the jabs and hooks
he landed. He saw it in your swollen,
cut eyes and bleeding mouth. But

like a cannonball you kept coming,
moving, bobbing and weaving,
hammering Ali's body, taking

his best shots, determined
to conquer and destroy,
even if it cost you your life.

Your pain was outside the ring,
in the cuts made by Ali's
caustic, razor-sharp words,

in the hard knocks of a Joe
who, to survive, had swept scraps
off a kosher slaughterhouse floor

and punched his way out
of the ghetto. Brave gladiator,
the Thriller was the least

of your gifts to us. Ali was wrong
to belittle your blackness. For
all his courage and conviction,

his greatness in the ring,
Ali would have been less
of a fighter and a champion

had you not endured pain.

Louisville

Always a homeboy, and home is
Louisville, Gateway to the South,
the city that believed a black boy
from Grand Avenue could be golden,
and a young black man could be
heavyweight champ of the world,

a city where Jim Crow decided
      where he lived and played,
      where and how he was educated,
      where he shopped and saw movies,
      where he worshipped,
      even the fountain he drank from,

the city where it all began:
      a stolen red and white Schwinn,
      Officer Joe Martin and Columbia Gym,
      a cocky, loudmouth black kid
who ran alongside school buses
but didn't care much about school,
a funny boy with a girlish face
big smile, and a bully's fist,

a city that is mother, father, brother
and friend of a prodigy
      possessed by gift and belief,
      loved and despised,
      revered and reviled,
      crowned and dethroned,

born to be a boxer,
a messenger,
a statesman,
a torch of hope.

Now, in Manila, 8,400 miles from home,
standing in the ring, victorious
in his hardest fought battle,
sweat dripping
in a shadow of death,

the world looking and listening,

Ali shouts out to Louisville,
proclaims it the greatest city of all time,
because he is the greatest champ
and a grateful native son,
and he knows
the city he loves
loves him back.

Big George

Kinshasa, Zaire. October 30, 1974.
Before the monsoon poured
and dawn draped the shaman moon,
two black American boxers stepped
into the ring, and the world stood still.
Foreman, heavyweight champion,
half-human, half-beast,
had devoured every opponent
without breaking a sweat.
Even Cosell had him picked.
So young, so strong, so fearless.
Barring a miracle, he said,
Ali will tumble from grace,
pulverized and mortified.

That day, with 60,000 looking on,
Foreman and Ali created art
on a canvas larger than a boxing ring,
larger than countries, continents,
and battlefields of war,
leaving indelible images and sounds
for every future generation
to sift out of ash and dust:

Ali bomaye, Ali bomaye!

Drums beating.
African children dancing.
Don King's porcupine hair.

Ruler Mobutu's portrait with leopard-skin hat
     hoisted above the arena.
The Godfather of Soul "doing it to death."

Ali doing the rope-a-dope.
Round after round, Foreman pounding
     Ali's body like a punching bag,
     sapping his own brute strength.
Ali's right hand landing,
     making sweat fly
     from Foreman's head,
     spinning him to the canvas
     like a top.

Ali bomaye, Ali bomaye!

Big George, years later, long after
the Rumble and monsoon rain,
you and Ali, by then,
two holy men of God,
embraced as friends. Humbly,
you called Ali *The Greatest*,
but take nothing from yourself, Champ.
You will always be a giant among fighters,
and a pillar of strength to black boys
who dare to dream of greatness.

Bundini

Bundini, we all know
much of Ali's greatness
was made by men in his corner:
Angelo Dundee, Ferdie Pacheco,
Wali Muhammad,
      but you brought the wind and fire:

    Float like a butterfly. Sting like a bee.
    Rumble young man rumble!

Court jester, prop master, voodoo prince,
armorbearer of the word,
and self-made magus, sometimes
you spoke in tongues, sometimes in parables,

but high up there, looking down
from His living room couch,

      "Shorty" knew how much
      your voice kept Ali's wings in the air.

Legend

My granddaddy used to say:
took God six days to make the world,
took Ali one day to turn it upside down.

He said Ali trained by wrestling alligators,
and cutting down trees with one hand.

One day Ali was shadowboxing
blindfolded at the bottom of Biscayne Bay
and wrestled two great white sharks.

He said he saw one fight when Ali came out
with one arm in a sling and TKO'd a guy
in the third round. Another time,

Ali came out in a straightjacket, the kind
Houdini used to wear, and about halfway
the first round the other fighter
was on his back taking the long count.

He said Ali had a secret knockout punch
that he used a couple of times, but his hands
were so fast if you blinked you missed it.

He said one night Ali was whipping a fellow
so bad that everybody's television started
smoking, then blew up in the middle of the fight.

Another time, Ali had been on the ropes
for 14 rounds, tough fight. 15th round,
he came out dancing, jabbing, hooking,
but his feet never touched the canvas,
not once. The poor fellow he beat said
it was like seeing Jesus walking on the sea.

Last Bell

Marciano was right.
You had the fever,
and couldn't quit

until you were beaten.
The fever had you.
Time and fire tested

your iron ribcage and jaw
but head blows took a toll.
The butterfly and bee

lost their wings.
The hummingbird lost
its speed and mid-flight

wizardry to dart, stop,
levitate, and back up
quicker than a blink.

Spinks, Holmes, and
Berbick were the last bell.
Three times heavy champ.

The killer syndrome
started its march, and
the mountain climb began.

Seeking God

The Torch

Muhammad, twenty years before you left us,
we saw you appear out of pitch-black darkness

on a mountainside and watched you step
slowly toward a blooming bush. Your hands,

trembling like a man twice your age, held
a lit torch and raised it high above your head,

as if you were saluting your maker, the first
and only lasting spirit of humankind.

You reached down and touched the bush
with your torch until an all-consuming fire

lit the midnight sky. Through tears, joy,
and adulation, through history and your life

flashing before us, we watched you stand
straight and strong until you became

our lives, our torch, our flaming, blooming
cauldron for dark, unsettling days.

Brother Malcolm

If I have any regret, it's that I didn't make things right
    between us, didn't tell you how much you meant to me
        and how sorry I was that our friendship ended.

Since that day in June of 1962, when Sam Saxon drove
    Rudy and me to Detroit to a Muslim rally to hear
        the Honorable Elijah Muhammad and meet you,

I wanted to learn more about the Muslim religion.
    Like a big brother, you took me under your wings
        and counseled me. You were a flame of fire

that lit my path to truth about the black man's power
    to control his own destiny and the white man's desire
        to permanently keep the black man in bondage.

Before meeting you, I had never heard a black man
    speak his mind with such boldness, without fear.
        I always had the utmost respect for your courage

to stand up for what is right, and for your integrity
    and wisdom. Most of all, you believed in me
        when few people did. You were one of the few

at ringside at my first Liston fight who believed
    I could win, because you knew that Allah
        had already ordained it. You were a true friend

and mentor, and for that I will always be grateful.
    The last time we spoke, meeting accidently in Ghana
        outside the hotel, you called my name, ready

to embrace and talk, but I spoke meanly, cold as ice,
    angry because you had called Allah's messenger,
        the Honorable Elijah Muhammad, a fraud,

and because you turned away from the truth
    that had set you free. In my mind and heart,
        you were a hypocrite and the enemy.

Blinded by loyalty to the Nation of Islam, I was
    still bitter toward you by the time of your death,
        unable to see that you, more than anyone,

helped me to find Allah's purpose in my life.
    In the end, we have crossed the same sands
        to kneel at the same altar and say

the same prayers. In true Islam, we are brothers.
    Until we meet again, As-Salaam-Alaikum,
        my friend. May the peace of God be with you.

Love,
Muhammad

Baghdad

After the ring, Parkinson's marching out front,
Ali, a prized pop culture commodity,
more recognized and revered than anyone
on the planet, takes to the political stage.
The Champ is punch drunk and delirious,
some black leaders say, when Ali endorses
Reagan for president in '84.

1990. Iraq invades Kuwait and takes 15
civilian American men hostage, uses them
as human shields against U.S. bomb targets
on Iraq facilities. In a defiant act against war,
Ali, the Muslim, shakes up the world,
goes to Baghdad on a mission from God.
The Bush White House calls his trip
loose-cannon diplomacy.

Ali takes to the streets of Baghdad,
signs autographs, prays in mosques,
and does magic tricks for school children.
Six days later, he meets with Iraq dictator
Saddam Hussein. The hostages are released
and go back to the U.S.A. In a whisper,
Ali says, *They don't owe me nothin'.*

Weeks later, the window of peace shuts.
The United States and Iraq go to war,
but 15 innocent men are home
with their families, grateful to God
and the Champ who set them free.

Parkinson's

I.

1996, twelve years after the diagnosis,
four months before the Summer Olympics,
CBS 60 Minutes, Sunday evening, prime time,
Ed Bradley interviewing the Champ.
Ali, wife Lonnie, and friend Howard Bingham
at a restaurant, outdoors,
seated for lunch, Bradley next to Ali,
the world looking on.

Ali, shoulders slumped, falls asleep.
Bingham calls Ali's name.
Bradley taps him on the arm.
Ali doesn't wake.

Lonnie explains:
I don't know. I wasn't there.
But ever since the Frazier fight
in Manila, Muhammad will—
it's sort of like—like narcolepsy.
He'll just start sleeping,
but he'll have these flashbacks.
And he'll have—it's like nightmares.
And his face will twist up,
like he's boxing,
and he'll throw punches at people.

Bradley, concern on his face,
stares at the Champ, still asleep.

Lonnie explains more:
And he does it at night sometimes.
Sometimes—I figured out the thing.
Whenever he starts snoring heavily,
I have to get out of the bed
because I know it's going to start.

Ali, eyes closed, remains in deep sleep.
He starts to move, makes a half-fist
with his right hand.

Bradley, visibly perplexed,
continues to stare the Champ down.
So, he's not putting on when he does this?

Lonnie, poker-faced:
No. This actually happens.
And the doctor told us not to really try
to wake him if that does happen
because he might end up with a heart attack
because it might frighten him.
So I don't. I just get up and move.

Bradley's eyes fixed on Ali.

Then, Ali, eyes still shut,
throws a left jab at Bradley but misses.
Bradley flinches, leans back.

Lonnie: *That's the hard part. You have to sort of . . .*

Suddenly, like a flash of lightning, Ali wakes,
snorts like a pig, and reaches for Bradley's arm,

Bradley, laughing: *You got me.*

II.

You could have gone underground,
been invisible to the world, but not Ali,
not in your biggest fight,
the one for your life.

No spoken word rhymes and predictions like:

    I might tremble and drag my feet,
    but ain't no disease I can't beat.

No braggadocious declarations of greatness like:

    Here I am world.
    I'm a baaaad man!
    I can't be beat.

No levitation and rope-a dope
in your mummy walk and mask face,
your slurred speech and trembling hands,
not in this fight.
As Bundini would say,

this is God's work. He's doing the talking.
He's calling the shots now.

Ali, that night in Atlanta in 1996,
when you stepped into the darkness
and lit the sky for a hurting world,
you gave Parkinson's your face,
your name,
your strength and courage,
your grace.

Afghanistan

In 2002, you would step slowly
onto the hallowed ground of war-torn Afghanistan
holding a bouquet of flowers in your trembling hands.

You would be given a royal welcome.
You would bring a message of peace and hope.
You would visit a school in a canvas tent
	and give volleyballs and jump ropes to young girls
	who were once forbidden to attend school.
You would visit a bakery in Kabul
	and receive a gift of bread from widows
	who had lost their husbands in war.
You would visit a boxing club made of mud walls,
	give gloves to young fighters,
	and prove that you can still punch the bag.
You would be inspired by the faith, strength
	and resiliency of the Afghan people,
	your brothers and sisters.
You would see God.

Three years later, you would stand in the White House
while a U.S. President, Viet Nam-era veteran
of the Air National Guard,
hung a Presidential Medal of Freedom
around your neck, calling you "a man of peace,"
the government that once tried and convicted you,
and sentenced you to prison for draft evasion.

If there was ever any doubt
that the God you worship
neither slumbers nor sleeps
that moment dispelled it.

Liminal

We know you talked with angels,
and made honey flow from flinty rock.
Once, with shackles binding your hands
and feet, you swam from the Gulf of Tonkin
to the Pacific Ocean. Liminal as Merlin,
the great enchanter, you dazzled us with magic.

Like Liston, Uncle Sam never saw
the silk handkerchief disappear
inside your glove,
and the steel ball you pulled from it.
You were Br'er Rabbit in the briar patch,
the sorcerer with hands quicker than a blink,
morphing into a butterfly, a bee, or a poet,
rope-a-doping against Goliath, then,
levitating inches above the ground.

Just when we thought we had seen
your best years and greatest triumphs,
another Ali emerged: the old man,
young in years but wise in knowledge
of truth and self. You whispered,
"Come walk with me up the mountain,"
and we did. Along the way, you bared
your infirmities and soul. You found
the most beautiful, precious, and
enduring stones, and, in silence,
spoke them to us.

Champ, time may tell, but could it be
that you were on Earth but not of it, a star,
near enough to be discovered and gazed,
yet too far to be known?

Son of Africa

What is Africa to me:
Copper sun or scarlet sea,
Jungle star or jungle track,
Strong bronzed men, or regal black
Women from whose loins I sprang
When the birds of Eden sang?
　　—Countee Cullen, "Heritage"

Brave, beautiful, gifted Ali,
deserving of the crown you wear
and the praise that cloaks you
like the lushness of our greenest fields,

　　your conviction to truth and justice
　　stirred the gods of our dreams.

Years ago, our men, women, and children
lined the streets, roofs, and treetops
to see the young American champion

　　who dared to call himself African
　　and Muslim and who let the glow

of his rays turn the eyes of the world
toward the beauty and greatness
of our beloved continent.

In our eyes you are one of us,
　　　cradled and fed by one bosom.

Even now, we sing and dance to your drum:
a song of freedom and resistance to war
that rings through the fire

　　　of your fervent silent prayers.

What you said of Mandela
can be said of you:

> *a man whose heart, soul and spirit*
> *could not be contained or restrained*
> *by racial and economic injustices,*
> *metal bars or the burden*
> *of hate and revenge.*

Finding God

"If God's with me, can't nobody be against me,"
22-year old Cassius shouted to the world,
minutes after he became heavyweight champ.
The long journey that followed, a war
of flesh and spirit, was solely
and uniquely his: being the greatest
at his God-given gift, defining who he was,
not who others wanted him to be,
him climbing toward wholeness
and the realization of his ultimate self.

When he reached the steep summit
of the mountain, night had fallen.
Dark clouds blanketed the stars and moon.
His body had grown weak and frail,
barely standing up
in the slashing wind and rain.
His past life, the seconds and minutes
moving, the days and years
he had yet to live, vanished.
He felt small, insignificant, then
invisible as the air he inhaled.

But Ali the Muslim lived
the Epistle of the Apostle James.
Standing atop the mountain,
in the blindness of a bitter, wintry storm,
his feeble hands let go of the snowy rock
and took hold of faith, full of breath

and countless acts of kindness.
He knelt and prayed. He reached back
to lift up children, to comfort the sick,
and sprinkle a little joy on the world.

In the Wake

Rain pouring all day.
Tributes, photo shots, film footage.

He floats.
He jabs.
He whups ass.
He mouths off.
He rhymes.
He defies.
He lights a torch.

The Greatest is dead.

I can't stop the rain.

Can't stop remembering a boy
dreaming, shadowboxing,
shuffling feet—me
pretending to be
Ali.

Remembrance

We gave him a farewell befitting of a king and faithful servant.
We remembered his greatness in the ring, the fire on his tongue
and in his heart, how he boldly said "no" to war and injustice,
and lit the world with a torch. We showered him with flowers
and tears, with praises and tributes. We traced the path of his
journey from Grand Avenue in Louisville to towns and cities
across America and countries around the globe, the journey
up his mountain to self-actualization, through the storied pages
of his large life, his triumphs and his defeats, through the lives
of those he helped to set free, those he comforted, brought
laughter to, cared for, and inspired. We honored him through
the eyes of a world that loved him: family, friends, strangers
and fans, those who touched him and were touched by him,
and in whose own lives he saw the great wonders of God.

Big Brother Muhammad

I never had the pleasure of meeting Muhammad Ali
or seeing him in person, but I've always admired him
as an athlete and a person who had the courage
to stand up for what he thought was right.
Muhammad was 10 years older than me.
In some way, I saw him as the big brother
that I didn't have. Like all the boys my age,
I thought he was exactly what he proclaimed
himself to be—The Greatest. I recited
his silly rhymes and shadowboxed,
pretending I was him, never any other fighter.

In April of 1967, when Muhammad refused
to be inducted, I was 14 years old.
That fall, I became a ninth grade student
at a white junior high school in the first year
of public school integration in my community.
I was one of only five black students there,
and one of two black males. I was the darker
skin Negro boy. That year was without a doubt
the loneliest and most depressing experience
of my life up to that point. A school day rarely
ended when I hadn't been treated in the most
degrading way, and hadn't felt humiliated
just because of the color of my skin.

My father was a great fan of boxing, especially
of Sugar Ray Robinson and Muhammad Ali.
Watching Friday night boxing on television

was like being in church on Sunday morning.
Except for home, I was seldom in places
where I heard grown people talk about Ali,
but I heard his story on the evening news.
Strangely, I felt a kinship: like me,
Muhammad was alone.
Of course, I knew we were different.
I was an ordinary, poor black boy
and he was heavyweight champ of the world.
I understood that our circumstances
and experiences were different. Still,
I felt that we had something in common.
We were black and living in a world
in which we were misunderstood
or not understood at all. People hated us
just for being ourselves. We weren't trying
to pretend or be somebody we weren't.
People just hated us for being who we were.
I felt proud that he was black
and had taken a stand against the Army,
and although I didn't understand
the Muslim religion or the Viet Nam war,
I admired Muhammad
for what he did and why he did it.
I never doubted his sincerity.

That was the cement of my bond
with Muhammad, then and over the years
that followed. My admiration for him grew
as I grew older. He is my greatest hero.

Muhammad Ali

When the final trumpet sounds, when we lay
our sword, shield, and heavy burden down
by the riverside, and we study war no more, this man,
this black boxer, this Muslim, this beautiful champion,
the greatest of all time, tried, convicted, and stripped
of his crown because he clung to his convictions,
because he denounced war and refused to kill
for a country that would not fight for him
to be free, this man of love, peace, and kindness,
this child of laughter, this seeker of God,
shall be remembered, not with words and films
and buildings built of stone, metal and glass alone,
but with the strength and courage that he inspires in us
to stand and sacrifice for what we believe is right.

Poetic pattern borrowed from "Frederick Douglass" by Robert
Hayden. Includes lyrics adapted from the Negro spiritual, "Down by
the Riverside."

Legacy

More than a boxer, the greatest of all time.
More than a man, among the rare and few,
who for the sake of freedom and justice
moved mountains and seas, and tilted

the axis of history, not with armies,
guns or vaults of gold, but with belief
in principles and the courage to fight
for them at the risk of losing their lives.

Ali, the boxer who ruled the ring,
the man adored by presidents, popes
and leaders around the world, who
gave his time and magic to children.

Ali, the man of God and messenger
for peace who had the gift of giving,
and who, for love, was not ashamed
to bare his brokenness to the world.

About the Author

John Warner Smith is the author of *Spirits of the Gods* (ULL Press, 2017), *Soul Be A Witness* (MadHat Press, 2016), and *A Mandala of Hands* (Kelsay Books–Aldrich Press, 2015). Smith's poems have appeared in numerous literary journals. He has been nominated for Pushcart Prizes and for the *Sundress Best of the Net Anthology*. A Cave Canem Fellow, Smith earned his MFA in Creative Writing at the University of New Orleans. He lives in Baton Rouge, Louisiana. His poetry can be found at www.johnwarnersmith.com.

Notes

I wrote my first poem about Muhammad Ali on June 4, 2016, the day after he died. At the time, I was working on another book project in which I wrote poems inspired by the visual art of Dennis Paul Williams. I had spent the prior week musing over several photographs of Dennis' art. In one of the paintings, I saw suffering and death, but I hadn't found a poem until I learned of Ali's death. The poem, "Ali," appears in that collection (*Spirits of the Gods*, ULL Press 2017) and was later retitled "In the Wake."

June f was a rainy day in Baton Rouge, and I was home alone, watching televised tributes to The Greatest. I cried through much of those broadcasts. It was the first time in my then 63 years that I had wept over the death of someone whom I had never met or known personally. In those images, I saw my own boyhood flashing before me. In some respects a part of me had also died.

The Greatest is dead.

I can't stop the rain.

Can't stop remembering a boy
dreaming, shadowboxing,
shuffling feet—me
pretending to be
Ali.

I didn't set out to write a book of poems about Muhammad Ali. One afternoon, months after his death, while sitting and staring blankly at a computer screen, I thought about him and wondered what poems had been written about him, the most written about athlete of all time. I was surprised and disappointed to find only a handful of poems, at least on the Internet. In that moment, the idea of the book was born.

But let me back up a bit. In early December 2015, I texted a Christmas list to my three children, hoping to make their shopping for Dad a little easier. On the list was a DVD of Ali's title fights. When I didn't get the gift, I discovered that it was one of several items in the text message that mysteriously "fell off" and was never received. By the time of Ali's death, I had purchased and often watched several DVDs of Ali's life and greatest fights. Today, the collection is quite extensive, including the videos that I immersed myself in while creating poems on Ali's life: *Muhammad Ali: The Greatest Collection; Muhammad Ali, Through the Eyes of the World; The Trials of Muhammad Ali; I Am Ali;* and *When We Were Kings.*

I began the project with poems about the storm of Ali's career —the time leading up to and during his legal battle with the U. S. government for failing to be inducted into the military. Early poems of the collection are of that period, 1965-1971. I am deeply indebted to Leigh Montville's bestselling book, *Sting Like A Bee,* for helping to kindle the fire for those late nights of reading and poem writing about the most tumultuous phase of Ali's career.

Ali's autobiography, *The Greatest, My Own Story,* also helped tremendously, enabling me to weave people and moments of Ali's youth and young adulthood into reflections of him as a rising boxing star and as a conscientious objector of war.

The Muhammad Ali Reader, a collection of essays and stories edited by Gerald Early and written by thirty-one authors, athletes, and social commentators (including Ali himself), provided a rich source of insight into Ali as a boxer and a man.

Several online sources were also helpful in guiding my

approach to capturing the influence of key people and events in Muhammad's life. While most of this information was biographical and historical in context, I found excerpts from *Blood Brothers: The Fatal Friendship Between Muhammad Ali and Malcolm X* by Randy Roberts and Johnny Smith (Basic Books, 2016) particularly helpful in writing the poem, "Brother Malcolm."

Poetry about Muhammad can easily be discovered in photographs taken of him, and, as the most photographed athlete of all time, there are many. Two sources were especially inspiring: *Muhammad Ali, The Tribute: 1942-2016*, by Sports Illustrated, and *Muhammad Ali Unfiltered*, a stunning collection of photographs produced by Jeter Publishing and edited by Maureen Cavanagh with a foreword by Lonnie Ali.

I read *The Soul of a Butterfly*, co-authored by Ali and his daughter Hana, late in the process, and it helped to validate my impressions of the spiritual journey and discovery of self that was the essence of Ali's greatness.

My goal was to tell the story of Muhammad Ali—boxer, man of faith, objector to war, and ambassador for peace—in poems that would teach younger and future generations of all races the significance and example that this "one life" has for their own abilities and capacities to bend history and change the world with personal courage and conviction to belief.

Achieving spiritual wholeness and oneness with divine purpose was the mountaintop that constantly stood before Ali. I believe that he was one of the few people of modern times who achieved that level of self-actualization. In the writing process, I discovered that the barest truths of Ali's struggles, defeats, and triumphs easily created their own beauty and art. I was blessed to be a vessel for that expression.

My thanks to Neil Leifer and Getty Images for affording me the opportunity to use the most iconic photograph of Muhammad on the book cover.

Very special, heartfelt thanks to Nikki Giovanni, Charles deGravelles, and Hana Ali for reading the manuscript and allowing me to share their kind words about the book with other readers.

Lastly, but certainly not least, I am deeply grateful to Bill Lavender, founder of Lavender Ink / Diálogos and a former teacher and advisor of mine at the University of New Orleans, for believing in this project and agreeing to publish it.